W9-BFW-755

COTE D'IVOIRE

[IVORY COAST]   *...in Pictures*

Courtesy of United Nations

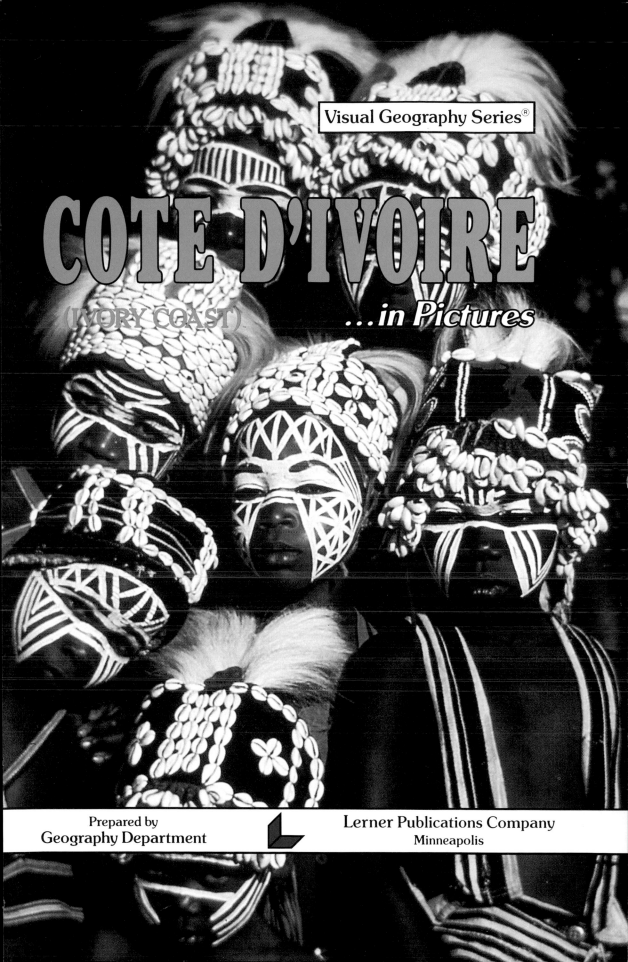

Visual Geography Series®

COTE D'IVOIRE

(IVORY COAST)

...in Pictures

Prepared by
Geography Department

Lerner Publications Company
Minneapolis

Independent Picture Service

A woman bathes her child in an Ivorian stream.

This is an all-new edition of the Visual Geography Series. Previous editions have been published by Sterling Publishing Company, New York City, and some of the original textual information has been retained. New photographs, maps, charts, captions, and updated information have been added. The text has been entirely reset in 10/12 Century Textbook.

LIBRARY OF CONGRESS CATALOGING-IN-PUBLICATION DATA

Côte d'Ivoire (Ivory Coast) in pictures.

(Visual geography series)
Rev. ed. of: The Ivory Coast in pictures / prepared by Albert Rossellini.
Includes index.
Summary: Text and photographs introduce the geography, history, government, people, and economy of the Ivory Coast.
1. Ivory Coast. [1. Ivory Coast] I. Rossellini, Albert. Ivory Coast in pictures. II. Lerner Publications Company. III. Title: Côte d'Ivoire in pictures. IV. Title: Ivory Coast in pictures. V. Series: Visual geography series (Minneapolis, Minn.)
DT545.22.C67   1988   966.6'8   87–17266
ISBN 0-8225-1828-7 (lib. bdg.)

International Standard Book Number: 0-8225-1828-7
Library of Congress Catalog Card Number: 87-17266

VISUAL GEOGRAPHY SERIES®

Publisher
Harry Jonas Lerner
Associate Publisher
Nancy M. Campbell
Senior Editor
Mary M. Rodgers
Editor
Gretchen Bratvold
Illustrations Editor
Karen A. Sirvaitis
Consultants/Contributors
Thomas O'Toole
Sandra K. Davis
Designer
Jim Simondet
Cartographer
Carol F. Barrett
Indexer
Sylvia Timian
Production Manager
Richard J. Hannah

Independent Picture Service

The Pyramid Building stands in the heart of the Plateau—Abidjan's business district.

Acknowledgments

Title page photo by Tourisme Côte d'Ivoire.

Elevation contours adapted from *The Times Atlas of the World*, seventh comprehensive edition (New York: Times Books, 1985).

1 2   3   4   5   6   7   8   9   10   97 96 95 94 93 92 91 90 89 88

As a ship steams into the port of Abidjan, fishermen mend their nets along the shore.

Courtesy of United Nations

Contents

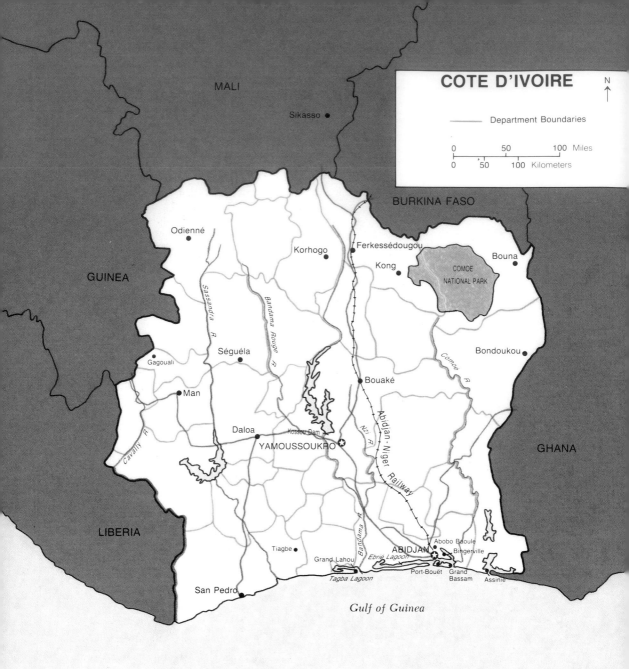

COTE D'IVOIRE

N

— Department Boundaries

0   50   100 Miles
0   50   100 Kilometers

MALI

Sikasso ●

BURKINA FASO

Odienné ●

Korhogo ●

Ferkessédougou ●

Bouna ●

GUINEA

Kong ●

COMOE
NATIONAL PARK

Séguéla ●

Bondoukou ●

Gagouali ●

Man ●

Bouaké ●

Daloa ●

Kossou Dam

YAMOUSSOUKRO ✪

GHANA

LIBERIA

Tiagbe ●

Abobo Baoule
Bingerville
ABIDJAN
Grand Lahou

Grand
Port-Bouët   Bassam

Ebrié Lagoon

Tagba Lagoon

Assinie

San Pedro ●

Gulf of Guinea

Sassandra R.
Bandama Rouge R.
Cavally R.
Nzi R.
Bandama R.
Comoe R.
Abidjan - Niger Railway

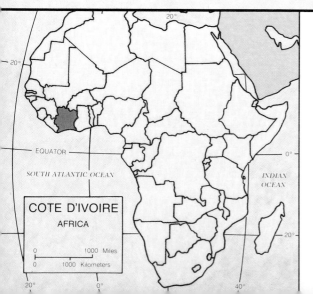

20°

20°

EQUATOR

0°

SOUTH ATLANTIC OCEAN

*INDIAN
OCEAN*

20°

COTE D'IVOIRE
AFRICA

0   1000 Miles
0   1000 Kilometers

40°   0°

METRIC CONVERSION CHART		
To Find Approximate Equivalents		
WHEN YOU KNOW:	**MULTIPLY BY:**	**TO FIND:**
AREA		
acres	0.41	hectares
square miles	2.59	square kilometers
CAPACITY		
gallons	3.79	liters
LENGTH		
feet	30.48	centimeters
yards	0.91	meters
miles	1.61	kilometers
MASS (weight)		
pounds	0.45	kilograms
tons	0.91	metric tons
VOLUME		
cubic yards	0.77	cubic meters
TEMPERATURE		
degrees Fahrenheit	0.56 (*after* subtracting 32)	degrees Celsius

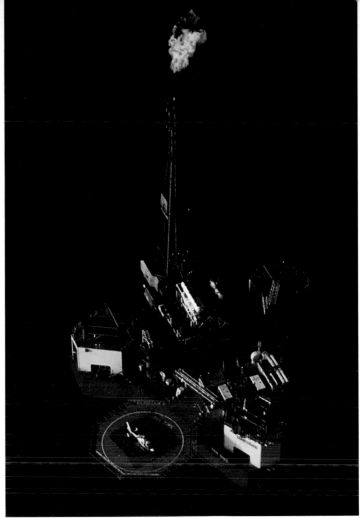

"Dan Duke," a drilling rig off the shores of Côte d'Ivoire, serves as a production site for an underwater oil field.

Introduction

Though far from the largest country in Africa, Côte d'Ivoire is a particularly important nation for those who study Africa and the Third World. As the meeting point of four major West African cultures, Côte d'Ivoire and its ethnic groups have become famous throughout the world for their artistic traditions.

Furthermore, Côte d'Ivoire often is cited as an example of a developing nation that has achieved substantial economic growth. This assessment is based on the nation's economic strategies, which encourage both foreign investment and expanded internal production. Côte d'Ivoire's success has been especially remarkable because, until it began producing petroleum from its offshore oil reserves in the 1970s, the country had no particular advantage over its African neighbors in raw materials.

The wealth created in Côte d'Ivoire has attracted workers from neighboring countries, as well as 50,000 French people who

7

Wooden statuettes, such as *Woman in Bondage,* are a traditional Ivorian art form.

have become permanent residents. About one-fourth of the black population consists of non-Ivorians, who take the most unskilled jobs in the country. While this arrangement gives the Ivorians a relatively privileged place on the social and economic ladder, it might also create problems. For example, non-Ivorians could easily become targets of anger should prosperity ever disappear and should jobs of any kind be hard to find.

Much of the attention given to Côte d'Ivoire has focused on the nation's president, Félix Houphouët-Boigny. He has been chief executive of the country since it gained independence in 1960. Although in his eighties, Houphouët-Boigny has refused to name a successor or even to approve a means of choosing one. Thus, an important topic of conversation in Côte d'Ivoire revolves around who will be the nation's next leader. There is a feeling in the country that change is needed, but there is also fear that the transition after Houphouët-Boigny may not be smooth.

Logs await shipment at the port of Abidjan. Côte d'Ivoire exports timber to several European countries.

The ivory tusks of elephants inspired Europeans to settle Côte d'Ivoire—where the animals were plentiful—in order to profit from trading their long, pointed teeth.

1) The Land

Côte d'Ivoire is roughly square-shaped and covers an area of about 124,000 square miles. Bounded on the south by 330 miles of the Gulf of Guinea, the country is slightly larger than the state of New Mexico. Other boundaries are formed by five adjacent nations—Liberia and Guinea to the west, Mali and Burkina Faso to the north, and Ghana to the east.

The boundaries of Côte d'Ivoire were drawn by the French, who established the area as a colony in 1893. The country takes its name—which in English means Ivory Coast—from the elephant ivory trade that flourished there in the late nineteenth and early twentieth centuries. Since that time, the elephant population has been greatly reduced, and the ivory trade has been outlawed.

The land is divided into three zones, which are notable more for differences in vegetation than for variations in landscape. Along the coast is a lagoon region; further north, west, and east lies a dense,

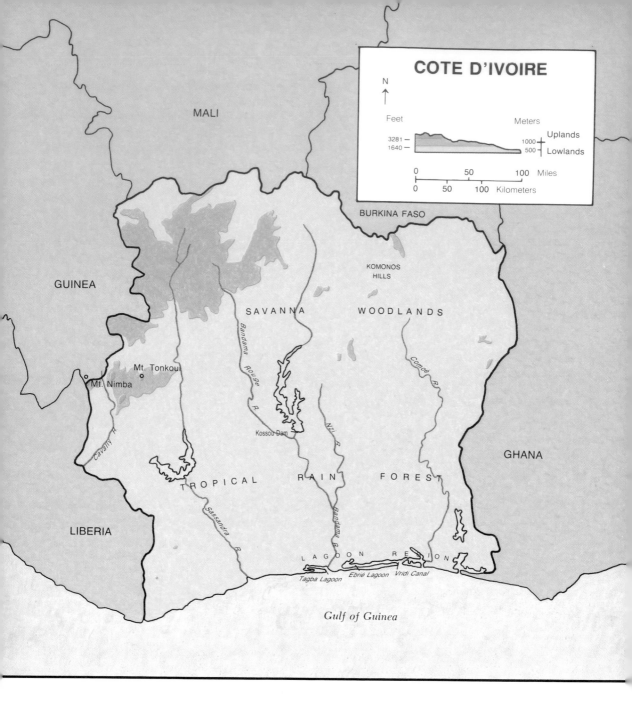

forested area. The rest of the country—
roughly two-thirds of it—is distinguished
by low woodlands.

The Lagoon Region

Composed of a very narrow piece of land,
the lagoon region extends along the coast
from the Ghanaian border to the mouth of
the Sassandra River. This generally flat
region is characterized by a large collection
of sandbars, which tend to inhibit coastal
navigation along the Gulf of Guinea, a
large inlet of the Atlantic Ocean. Ocean
currents and pounding surf have created
the sand barriers, which have closed

almost all of the river mouths that feed into the gulf. Shallow lagoons have formed between the sandbars and the true Ivorian coastline. The lagoons are sometimes connected to one another by small canals, most of which were built under the colonial French administration.

A few of the large rivers within Côte d'Ivoire do manage to reach the coast to empty into the Gulf of Guinea. Where this emptying happens, broad estuaries (channels where the river meets the sea) may extend for several miles.

Vegetation surrounding the lagoons is mostly of the woodland type—a change from the dense rain-forest that existed in the area before it was cleared for plantations. Around the swampier lagoons, mangrove thickets still thrive.

The Rain-Forest

The Ivorian rain-forest is at the northernmost extremity of a belt of tropical vegetation that runs from west to east in the middle of the African continent. A section of this broad piece of forested land occupies about one-third of Côte d'Ivoire. Located just north of the lagoon region, the rain-forest extends from Liberia on the west to Ghana on the east. Its northern boundary dips deeply in the center and lies about 75 miles north of the port of Grand Lahou.

Except where the forest has been disturbed by human habitation or by efforts to exploit it as a natural resource, it flourishes unchecked. Slash-and-burn techniques have been used to clear some of the land for banana, pineapple, and oil palm plantations. This method of land development has caused once-lush portions of the northern forest to become grassy woodlands. The western and eastern sections, however, are largely untouched.

The rain-forest is characterized by gently rolling terrain, with only a few distinctive heights. The only stark relief on the

The traditional, grass-covered dwellings in a northern Ivorian village fit naturally into the surrounding landscape.

Columns driven into a lagoon form the foundations for homes in Tiagbe, a village west of Abidjan.

landscape of this region is west of the Sassandra River, near the Liberian border. Here, a ridge of highlands rises near the city of Man and continues in a northwestern direction toward Odienné and Korhogo. Côte d'Ivoire's highest peak—Mount Nimba (6,069 feet)—rises at the point where Liberia, Guinea, and the Côte d'Ivoire meet.

The Savanna Woodland Area

The savanna woodland region is the southern end of another vegetation zone that begins in the deserts of northern Africa. In Côte d'Ivoire, this region is characterized by short grasses and isolated groups of trees.

The terrain here rises very gradually in a northward direction until it reaches the border of Guinea. At this point, the western landscape again meets the highlands

that began near Man. Mount Tonkoui (4,260 feet) dominates the horizon, but other, lower summits—between 1,000 and 2,000 feet above sea level—are also visible.

Rivers

Four main rivers—the Bandama, the Sassandra, the Comoé, and the Cavally—flow in Côte d'Ivoire. They all have their sources in the north and run almost directly south, emptying into the lagoons and finally into the Gulf of Guinea.

The easternmost river—the Comoé—originates in Burkina Faso and empties into the Ebrié Lagoon near Grand Bassam. Shallow vessels can navigate its length for only about 30 miles.

The basin of the Bandama River includes the level, central part of Côte d'Ivoire. As the main artery of a three-part river system, the Bandama is the largest and most important waterway in the country. The western Bandama Rouge River and the eastern Nzi River join the Bandama in the south to form a single waterway for the last 60 miles of its journey to the Gulf of Guinea. The river empties its waters into the sea at Tagba Lagoon, opposite Grand Lahou. Another feature of the Bandama is the new hydroelectric complex at Kossou.

The Sassandra River flows directly south from its source near Odienné. A narrow estuary that extends about 10 miles inland provides a coastal outlet for the Sassandra. The last of the four rivers—the Cavally—has its headwaters in the Nimba Mountains of Guinea and forms part of the Ivorian-Liberian border.

None of these rivers is fully navigable because of rapids. Moreover, due to seasonal rainfall, the rivers fluctuate between dry streambeds and surging torrents, depending on the time of year. Consequently, careful calculations are needed to take advantage of high water for navigation.

Independent Picture Service

Since its completion in 1972, the hydroelectric power station at Kossou (left) near Yamoussoukro has doubled Côte d'Ivoire's electricity production. During the project's construction (below), roughly 75,000 residents resettled into 70 villages, abandoning 650 square miles of land. The area filled with water, forming an artificial lake when the Bandama River was dammed.

Courtesy of United Nations

13

Flora and Fauna

The lush forest zone produces a great variety of plants, from huge trees to shrubs, vines, and herbs. Among the trees are giant dracaenas, bombax trees, oil palms, raffia palms (which yield a commercially valuable fiber), and many species that contain latex—the natural source of rubber. In dry climatic zones of Côte d'Ivoire, the distinctive baobab tree thrives because its trunk is able to store water for long periods of time.

Other native trees of commercial value are the kola (which yields kola nuts), the West African *Coffea liberica* tree, the African mahogany, and the cedar. Oil palms and coconut palms are abundant along the coast, and orchids and ferns not only cover the forest floor but also cling to the trunks and branches of forest trees.

Herds of elephants still roam the southwestern forest region, which is also home to the small, red buffalo. A number of species of antelope and wild hogs, as well as leopards, hyenas, and a variety of smaller animals are found throughout Côte d'Ivoire. Hippopotamuses visit shallow lakes, and monkeys are especially abundant in the dense forests. In northeastern Côte d'Ivoire, stretching over 2.5 million acres of wooded savanna, lies Comoé National Park, which has elephants, antelope, buffalo, lions, and leopards within its boundaries.

The baobab's enormous trunk stores a reserve of water that nourishes the tree during the dry season.

Côte d'Ivoire began establishing game reserves in the 1950s to protect the nation's wildlife. In their natural habitats, animals, such as giraffes *(top)* and lions *(bottom)*, roam the national parks in safety.

Semi-aquatic hippopotamuses spend much of their day almost entirely submerged in water. They can remain completely underwater for as long as 25 minutes.

Cacao pods grow from the trunks of cacao trees in the southern forest region. Côte d'Ivoire produces 450,000 tons of cacao each year.

Because the lagoon region offers so many different environments, it plays host to a variety of birds, such as ducks, egrets, herons, and terns. Birds of the jungle—including parrots and plantain eaters, or touracos—often have bright feathers. In addition to these year-round winged creatures, a large population of European migratory birds flies south to spend the winter in Côte d'Ivoire.

The main Ivorian reptile is the crocodile, which is frequently found in muddy streams and lagoons. Common snakes include mambas, cobras, and pythons.

Climate

The southern half of the country is characterized by a tropical climate—temperatures are constantly at around 80° F and humidity levels are high. The land is drenched from April to June—the long rainy season—and again in October and November—the short rainy season. Rainstorms are brief but frequent, and they unleash enormous quantities of water. In some places along the coast, particularly in areas of both the southwest and the southeast, the average annual rainfall reaches 80 inches.

Crocodiles thrive in Côte d'Ivoire's many lagoons and keep cool by immersing themselves in mud.

During the rainy season fog shrouds Man, a town that lies 250 miles northwest of Abidjan.

In Adjame, a subdivision of Abidjan, housing and services have been unable to keep pace with substantial increases in the quarter's population.

The northern climate is much drier and has greater differences in temperature. Only one rainy season occurs in the north, from May to October, where the average yearly rainfall is 47 inches.

Capital Cities

At the turn of the twentieth century, fishermen paddled canoes through the waters surrounding Abidjan, a peaceful fishing village of perhaps 700 inhabitants.

In addition to being the new capital of Côte d'Ivoire, Yamoussoukro is a planned city, which means that architects and engineers carefully laid out the streets and buildings for maximum efficiency and attractiveness.

The many skyscrapers of Abidjan's cityscape illustrate its economic growth in recent years.

In the succeeding decades, cargo ships and sleek passenger liners churned up those same waters. Today modern gray-and-white buildings overshadow this major city's thoroughfares, which are crammed with cars, taxis, and buses.

Abidjan has five subdivisions, which are connected by superhighways and two bridges. One of these sections, known as the Plateau, has graceful, modern architecture that rises above the lagoons and boasts office buildings, elegant restaurants, and shops. The Plateau is the administrative and financial heart of the city and of the country. Cocody and Marcory, both situated east of the Plateau, are wealthy areas, whose residents live in fine houses and enjoy well-tended gardens.

The majority of the city's 1.8 million people are concentrated in the crowded subdivisions of Treichville and Adjame. The residents—half of whom are Ivorians and half of whom are other West Africans —live in ethnically distinct districts that maintain traditional ties and customs.

In contrast to the wealth and comfort evident in Cocody and Marcory, Treichville and Adjame have lower standards of living. Housing in these suburbs has not kept pace with the large numbers of people

Palm trees crowd the yards of Cocody, a suburb of Abidjan, where wealthy Ivorians and Europeans live.

The rock formation known locally as *Le Dent de Man* (Man's Tooth) is a familiar landmark of eastern Côte d'Ivoire.

moving in from rural areas, and slums of makeshift living quarters have resulted.

Yamoussoukro has been the official administrative and political capital of the country since 1983. The actual governmental bureaucracy remains in Abidjan. Birthplace of President Houphouët-Boigny, Yamoussoukro was planned as a model urban center. Just outside of town lies the president's plantation—a sprawling agricultural experiment on which he intended to grow every Ivorian crop and to explore new possibilities for farming improvements. The plantation, like the town's elaborate party headquarters and luxury hotel, is seldom used to its full capacity.

Secondary Cities

Located 245 miles north of Abidjan, Bouaké (population 640,000) lies in the middle of the country, on the southern edge of the savanna. A bustling agricultural and industrial town, Bouaké is the site of the nation's oldest and largest textile factory, as well as of food-processing plants and of factories that produce soap, cigarettes, chemicals, and automobiles. An impressive mosque bears witness to a

Independent Picture Service

The ornate minarets, or towers, of a mosque in Bouaké characterize the city's mostly Muslim population, which is descended from the Dyula.

large Muslim population, many of whom are descended from the Dyula who established Bouaké many years ago as a vital link in a major commercial route.

Man (population 450,000) lies near the Liberian and Guinean borders and is tied to the north and middle of the country by 15 major roads. The city is the administrative and commercial capital of western Côte d'Ivoire. In addition, the natural beauty of the area—set among mist-covered highlands—has recently made Man a major tourist attraction.

Korhogo, the main city of the northern area, and Ferkessédougou are set in the savanna lands. Both have predominantly Muslim populations but are also centers of the non-Islamic Senufo, who are the second largest ethnic group in Côte d'Ivoire. Agricultural staples—groundnuts (peanuts), sorghum (a cereal grain), rice, and yams—are grown in these regions. With its new sugarcane plantations and refinery, Ferkessédougou has attempted to grow and process enough sugar to become the country's main supplier. The attempt so far has been unsuccessful.

Courtesy of Tom O'Toole

Yamoussoukro's Hôtel Président—one of the largest inns in Côte d'Ivoire—is rarely filled to capacity.

2) History and Government

The oldest traces of human occupation in the modern-day territory of Côte d'Ivoire date back about 3,500 years. These remains include discarded shells and stone tools that have been found along the edges of the coastal lagoons and of the major river estuaries.

From the tenth century onward, population growth, trade motives, and perhaps the spread of Islam—the Muslim religious faith—pressured African groups to leave their homes in the northern parts of the continent. Some of these groups moved south to begin independent communities in the area that is now Côte d'Ivoire.

Early Immigrations

Until the fifteenth century most people dwelling in the southern half of the country lived as hunters and gatherers in small, relatively isolated groups. Thick forests, fairly small populations, and difficult coastal areas with dangerous surf allowed the inhabitants of Côte d'Ivoire to escape most of the slave trade of the succeeding centuries.

Malinke peoples migrating from northwestern Africa in the sixteenth century pushed into the territory of the Senufo, who had themselves fled to the area earlier to escape from the Mali Empire. At this time, the Senufo lived in farming villages and towns from Sikasso (in Mali) to Bouaké. Under the gradual advance of the Malinke, the Senufo were forced to move south and east.

Some of the northern Malinke peoples were traders who were searching for kola nuts and other forest products. These merchants—bringing with them the Muslim faith—spread across the savanna to Bondoukou and established major trading routes to the Niger River and beyond.

In the seventeenth and eighteenth centuries, under pressure from more powerful peoples to the east, two Akan peoples—the Agni and the Baule—emigrated to Côte d'Ivoire from present-day Ghana. The Agni settled around Bondoukou, while the Baule crossed the Comoé River and settled in the middle of the country.

In essence, then, the many ethnic groups now residing in Côte d'Ivoire are historically descended from refugee populations, which fled to Ivorian land to escape pressures in their own territories. As a result, the history of Côte d'Ivoire is inseparable from that of West Africa until Côte d'Ivoire's colonization by the French.

French Influence Begins

The Portuguese and other Europeans touched the coast of Côte d'Ivoire as early as the fourteenth century. It was not until 1637, however, that the first French visitors landed at Assinie. The newcomers were missionaries; three of the original five

died soon after being exposed to a local infection. The French founded settlements at Grand Bassam and Assinie, but, because of the difficulty in maintaining these new communities, they lasted only a few years. Poor anchorages discouraged further commercial and missionary attempts to establish posts along the hazardous Ivorian coast for the next 200 years.

Then, in 1842—as part of the general European scramble for colonial possessions —the French government launched a policy of intensive exploration of the West African coast with the idea of acquiring valuable territories. This policy led to meetings at Grand Bassam and Assinie between French emissaries and local leaders. In the resulting treaties, the French promised to protect the villages and to pay an annual rent. As their part of the treaties, the Africans agreed to

The Malinke brought the Islamic faith to Côte d'Ivoire, which is now over 60 percent Muslim. This mosque—made entirely of mud—stands in the northern town of Kong, one of the great cities of African Islam.

trade only with the French and to allow them to establish forts.

From the French point of view, this arrangement soon became unsatisfactory. There was little trade, and the military outposts were hard to defend. Disinterest on the part of the French government and losses in the Franco-Prussian War between 1870 and 1871 led the French to abandon their forts in West Africa. The area was turned over to private French merchants, who were allowed to make further contracts with local leaders in the name of France.

In 1885 the Berlin Conference of European powers established spheres of influence in Africa for European countries. If France wanted to lay claim to any area on the African continent, it had to develop its presence there immediately. Renewed French interest in Côte d'Ivoire resulted, and the French government took back direct control of the forts.

Colonization

In 1893 Côte d'Ivoire became a French colony headed by a French governor, with an administrative organization sent from France. The colonial government was located in Grand Bassam. The commanding military officer of the colony, Captain Louis-Gustave Binger (Bingerville was named after him), began to establish inland posts and to define the borders more precisely.

Some resistance to colonization was inevitable, but the French military forces

Courtesy of Phil Porter

Built between 1903 and 1912 and set in a large garden, the colonial Governor's Palace in Bingerville reflects French architectural influence. Today the residence is used as an orphanage.

had not anticipated the well-trained armies of the Malinke leader Samory Touré. From 1879 to 1898 Samory and his army raged through Guinea, Mali, Burkina Faso, Ghana, and Côte d'Ivoire, at times depleting the French forces with skillful military maneuvers. At one point, Samory established his rule in northern Côte d'Ivoire between Odienné and Bouna, completely annihilating and plundering such towns as Bouna and Kong.

In 1898 Samory tried to lead his troops across the mountainous region of Man and into Guinea in the middle of the rainy season. In a short time the weather took its toll, and the Malinke leader's army was reduced to half of its original size. Captured on September 29, 1898, Samory was exiled to Gabon in western equatorial Africa, where he died in 1900.

Colonial Policies

Eventually, the French government organized its overseas African colonies into two large federations. One of them— French West Africa—included the area of Côte d'Ivoire. (The other federation was French Equatorial Africa.) Along with colonial reorganization in the early 1900s came African resentment toward unjust colonial policies.

Although local African leaders were responsible for the day-to-day administration of their villages, France considered the African populations to be French *sujets* (subjects). The French obliged all of its sujets to submit to the *corvée*—forced labor on public works projects—and adult males were drafted for military service. Furthermore, the colonial legal system allowed suspected criminals to be imprisoned without trial.

The French government encouraged European settlers—especially farmers— to immigrate by offering them five-year freehold grants for coffee and cacao plantations. African farmers resented the preferential treatment given to the foreigners.

The policy of French colonial administrators largely allowed ethnic groups to retain their structure and local traditions. Thus, Dan peoples of the mountainous Man region still built vine bridges *(above)*, and other groups continued to produce handwoven cloth *(below)* using techniques that had been employed for many centuries.

FRANCE

GREAT BRITAIN

PORTUGAL

GERMANY

ITALY

SPAIN

BELGIUM

INDEPENDENT STATES

Artwork by Larry Kaushansky

By the late nineteenth century, European powers had carved the continent of Africa into areas of influence. Present-day Côte d'Ivoire was included in the region called French West Africa. Map information taken from *The Anchor Atlas of World History*, 1978.

From its practice of enlisting the support of entire villages, the PDCI gathered its political strength.

The antagonism decreased in 1937, when a more liberal French government became sympathetic to the needs of the Africans, allowing them, for example, to organize a trade union for the first time. The new government also restricted the use of the corvée.

During World War II, when the pro-Nazi Vichy regime took over the government of France, liberals in the French colonies were driven out. Discrimination and enforced labor were again permitted in Côte d'Ivoire by the colonial administration, which took its orders from the Vichy government. The 60 Ivorian ethnic groups became united in reactions of resentment.

The PDCI and the Road to Independence

In 1944 a Baule leader named Félix Houphouët-Boigny, along with other important planters, organized the African Agricultural Union (SAA). This anti-Vichy organization sought to secure better prices for African products, to eliminate prac-

tices that benefited European farmers, and to abolish forced labor. Its leaders, in particular Houphouët-Boigny, became associated in the public's mind with the independence movement.

After World War II, a more liberal administration in France offered Côte d'Ivoire its first opportunity to present its political concerns in Paris. In 1945 Houphouët-Boigny—by then a symbol of West African unity—was elected as representative to the French legislature.

The young Ivorian representative presented a bill to the legislature that proposed the abolition of forced labor in France's colonial possessions. The law passed, and Houphouët-Boigny quickly became a leader in African politics. An alliance between the SAA and organized supporters of Houphouët-Boigny resulted in the founding of the Parti Démocratique de Côte d'Ivoire (PDCI), which dominated the political scene and dictated the course of events leading to Ivorian independence.

The massive power that the PDCI now enjoys can be traced back to its beginnings

27

in 1946. When the party was being formed, it sought not to recruit single members but rather whole villages at a time. Other villages of the same ethnic group were then brought into the party. A person became a party member not by individual choice but because that person had a particular ethnic origin. This structure made it possible for the party to mobilize large amounts of support.

The movement spread quickly, and soon the party embraced the majority of ethnic groups in Côte d'Ivoire. The party rose in stature and power as the Ivorians were led to believe that those who opposed the PDCI also opposed unity.

The Colonial Response to the PDCI

Between 1946 and 1950, opposition parties were encouraged by the colonial administration, which viewed the rapid advance-ment of the African cause with some uneasiness. As a result of this outside pressure, the PDCI became internally more solid and continually harassed the colonial government. During this time of conflict, however, the party began to lose its popular support.

Houphouët-Boigny and the PDCI saw that they could regain public confidence by establishing good relations with the colonial administration. Thus, under French pressure, opposition groups—such as the Communist party—were either eliminated or absorbed. Prices soared, the economy improved dramatically, and Houphouët-Boigny and the PDCI benefited from a broadly based network of support.

Meanwhile, Houphouët-Boigny was gaining influence in the French national legislature. In 1956 he became one of the first African cabinet ministers in the French government.

This run-down colonial building in Grand Bassam once housed French staff members of the colonial administration in Côte d'Ivoire.

Félix Houphouët-Boigny studied medicine in Dakar, Senegal, before returning to Yamoussoukro to work as a doctor and to manage his coffee plantation. Unlike the leaders of other West African nations, the president encouraged a good postindependence relationship with France.

In the 1960s Félix Houphouët-Boigny cemented relations with France by meeting with French president Charles de Gaulle.

Independence

Armed with such strong political power, Houphouët-Boigny secured grants of French aid for Côte d'Ivoire and attracted European business interests to the colony. Having harmonized French policy with the political and commercial growth of Côte d'Ivoire, Houphouët-Boigny came to be known as the main force within the country. His party, the PDCI, became synonymous with the Ivorian people. As a result, independence came peacefully in 1960. The occasion did not mark an end to close relations with France but rather became the

The state coat of arms of Côte d'Ivoire features two palm trees surrounding a shield underneath a setting sun. The elephant on the shield is the symbol of the PDCI. The elephant's ivory tusk represents the once-important trade item that gave the country its name.

starting point for greater commercial exchange and continued political agreement between the two countries.

Since becoming president in 1960, Houphouët-Boigny has almost single-handedly directed the policy of Côte d'Ivoire. His design is primarily geared toward material wealth, which the president believes will generate improvements in social conditions. Houphouët-Boigny has taken whatever measures he has thought necessary—occasionally including ones

that have been violent or outside the law—to ensure the stability of his regime.

Modern Political Tensions

Houphouët-Boigny's greatest opposition usually comes from student organizations, which are critical of the one-party system, of capitalism, of limited freedom, and of other aspects of the government. When a hostile student organization began a strike at the University of Abidjan in May 1969,

Houphouët-Boigny ordered the army to occupy the university and to arrest some 400 students. Most of the students were released after signing a pledge to refrain from further political activity without the guidance of the PDCI.

In the 1980s antigovernment groups were established in Abidjan and in larger towns. One organization—the Front Populaire Ivorien (Popular Ivorian Front), founded in August 1983—was particularly strong among teachers, students, and some sectors of the civil service. This group marked the first time in many years that opposition to Houphouët-Boigny had gathered into a single organization.

Part of the political tension in Côte d'Ivoire comes from the PDCI belief that a strong economy is more important than political goals. For example, to the dismay of some Ivorians, Côte d'Ivoire continues to support trade with South Africa—a country whose policies of racial separateness have limited the number of its African trading partners.

Houphouët-Boigny's commitment to seeking agreement rather than conflict has produced massive foreign investments, though this approach has not always pleased the more politically oriented heads of neighboring countries. Overwhelming all other concerns, however, is the continuing uncertainty about Houphouët-Boigny's successor. The president—reportedly born in 1905—has even refused to name a vice president, and the speculation about

The up-to-date port facilities of the Vridi Canal, just outside of Abidjan, demonstrate Houphouët-Boigny's belief in a strong economy first and social issues second.

The Ivorian government is involved in many cooperative schemes that are meant to bring social benefits, education, and work to Ivorians. Here, members of La Fraternelle Cooperative in Abidjan build a cottage *(above)*, and workers at a large mill, also in the city, stack sacks of flour *(below)*.

the aftermath of his rule continues to produce political tension.

The Government

The national legislature of Côte d'Ivoire adopted a constitution on October 31, 1960. The document provided for a strong presidency, for a degree of separation between the executive and legislative branches, and for an independent judiciary.

In theory the constitution provides for the free election of both the president and members of the legislature every five years by direct voting procedures. In practice, however, free choice is exercised only within very strict limits. The voter does not cast a ballot for an individual but rather for a list of candidates drawn up by the president and a few top advisers.

Since its founding in 1946, the PDCI has dominated the Ivorian government. All 70 members of the Ivorian legislature, all administrative heads, and most of the voting public belong to the party.

Filling a double role—as president of the PDCI and as president of Côte d'Ivoire—Houphouët-Boigny has enjoyed a degree of unquestioned power that is rarely seen in democratic republics. Major decisions—in any sphere of government—are not made without first consulting him. Usually, he and his cabinet officers initiate legislation. Although the legislature has the right to veto the president's bills, it has never done so.

Reuters/Bettman Newsphotos

In December 1985 French president François Mitterrand (right) welcomed Félix Houphouët-Boigny to Paris for a three-day meeting—part of the continuing contact between Côte d'Ivoire and France.

A white-turbaned member of the Lobi, a group that lives in the northeast, is surrounded by some of his children and several of his wives.

3) The People

Only since the mid-1960s have the people of Côte d'Ivoire—who now number 10.8 million—begun to develop a national consciousness. Thus, they now consider themselves first of all as Ivorians and only secondarily as members of a particular ethnic group. The social evolution that has taken place in Côte d'Ivoire—from a mixed collection of peoples to a single nation with a sense of unity—is one of the social accomplishments of contemporary African history.

Before the coming of the French, the land that is now Côte d'Ivoire was inhabited by at least 60 ethnic groups, each with a distinct language and set of customs. This human mosaic was formed by the juncture of four cultures, which were radically different from each other in terms of geographical origin, history, customs, and language. Each of these four groups—the Atlantic East, the Atlantic West, the Voltaic, and the Manding—was centered outside of Côte d'Ivoire. The groups, therefore, had more in common with the people of surrounding countries than with their fellow Ivorians.

The Atlantic East

The most prominent groups of the Atlantic East are the Agni and the Baule. Originally part of the Akan kingdoms in adjacent Ghana, these two groups separated and migrated west to Côte d'Ivoire 200 to 300 years ago.

AGNI

When the Agni separated from the Akan and moved into Côte d'Ivoire, they brought with them the tradition of inherited kingdoms. Thus, as they settled in the eastern portions of Côte d'Ivoire, between the Comoé River and the border of the modern nation of Ghana, they established four royal domains. One of these—the Sanwi kingdom—attempted in 1950 to declare itself independent from Côte d'Ivoire. The Agni are a Kwa-speaking group that numbered 200,000 people in the mid-1980s.

BAULE

According to legend, the Baule, originally residing in Ghana, were led by a wise and celebrated queen named Abraha-Pokou. The queen ordered that a surplus of cereals be stored in case of famine. When famine did come, the people were attacked by ruthless enemies. Rather than forfeit the food, the queen led her people west into Côte d'Ivoire. They reached the Comoé River, which they found impossible to cross. A sacrifice to the gods was necessary, and Queen Abraha-Pokou sacrificed

Independent Picture Service

Accompanied by his advisers, a traditional leader, or chief, of the Baule meets with the people of his village.

her own child. In recognition of this gift, the trees bent down across the river to form a bridge, and the queen led her people into a new land of safety and peace. Thus it is said that the word *baule* means "the little one dies." The legend demonstrates a reverence for nature that persists among the Kwa-speaking Baule, who have gained a reputation as the best farmers in Côte d'Ivoire.

The Atlantic West

A number of small ethnic groups—including the Bete and the Wobe—are found in the southwestern forest region. The ancestry of some of these peoples probably goes back more than 1,000 years in Côte d'Ivoire. The majority of these groups and their descendants have lived in small farming villages for most of the last 500 years, though some members along the

Courtesy of United Nations

In Gagouali, a town in western Côte d'Ivoire, a woman and her children relax in a handwoven hammock.

Two Senufo carry the body of a recently deceased member of their people to his burial site. Four days of communal mourning will follow the dead man's burial.

coast have a reputation as excellent fishermen.

The million or so people of the southwestern forest, who live far away from major population centers, tend to be less integrated into the national life of Côte d'Ivoire. Pushed south and west by more powerful groups from the north and the east, they still mistrust the authority of the central government.

Voltaic Group

The Voltaic group is multinational, extending across northern Côte d'Ivoire, northern Ghana, and Burkina Faso. Within Côte d'Ivoire, the major representatives of the group are the Senufo, a Gwa-speaking people.

The Senufo came to the area from farther north in the sixteenth century and formed various subgroups across the savanna. These peoples finally settled in Korhogo, Séguéla, Odienné, and Kong.

Peaceful and concerned chiefly with farming, the Senufo were exploited and pushed back by more military-oriented groups, such as the Malinke. During the invasions of the Malinke sovereign Samory Touré, whole Senufo villages were destroyed.

The Senufo now reside in north central Côte d'Ivoire, principally around Korhogo and Ferkessédougou. Most Senufo still feel a strong relationship to the land and to their agricultural way of life.

Manding

In the last several thousand years the Manding peoples have been responsible for two great imperial states—the Ghana and Mali empires—both of which were developed in what is today the Republic of Mali. The Manding culture once was divided into three main groups—the Malinke, the Bambara, and the Dyula. It is no longer easy to distinguish them, however, because

A woman in Abidjan balances her belongings on her head while carrying a baby in a sling on her back.

their language—Mande—and customs have become increasingly similar. In Côte d'Ivoire, most members of the Manding group are called Dyula.

Historically, the Dyula have been traders (*dyula* means "trader" in Mande). Their language is the local commercial tongue in many West African countries, and they are known as merchants throughout Côte d'Ivoire. Strong believers in Islam, the Dyula account for most of the nation's two million Muslims.

Minority Populations

More than two million people from other countries have taken up permanent residence in Côte d'Ivoire. They are drawn to the country because, by African standards, it is a rich land. Many of the new arrivals come from Burkina Faso—a relatively poor and barren region. They are willing to work at any job and to accept the lowest pay. Large numbers of people from Mali, Ghana, Guinea, Togo, and Benin also reside in Côte d'Ivoire.

Lebanese—who have run businesses in West Africa for a long time—live in cities

This outdoor laundry business near Abidjan is highly organized. The laundry is collected from house to house, and cleaning stations, located on large rocks, are used on a strict rotation basis.

This map shows the general distribution of the main ethnic groups in Côte d'Ivoire. Kwa-speakers include the Agni, Baule, Kru, and Guere, while the Malinke and the Dan are Mande-speaking peoples. The Senufo speak the Gur language, which has its roots in the Volta River area of Burkina Faso.

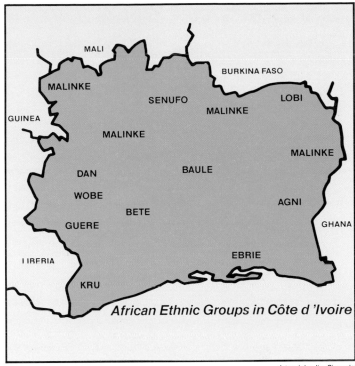

African Ethnic Groups in Côte d 'Ivoire

throughout Côte d'Ivoire, operating grocery stores, hotels, and restaurants. Europeans—mostly from France—number more than 200,000, and the majority reside in the commercial hubs of Abidjan and Bouaké. They are most frequently engaged in government service, missionary work, education, and commerce.

Language

Côte d'Ivoire—with its 60 different ethnic tongues—has one of the highest numbers of verbal communication forms in Africa. All of its ethnic languages can be classified as part of the Niger-Congo family. Of the eight major branches in this family, four are represented in Côte d'Ivoire.

Four language groups—Atlantic, Mande, Gur, and Kwa—are distributed throughout the land roughly according to the four cultural regions. It is doubtful, however, that any single tongue—including French,

the official language—can be understood by more than about one-tenth of the population. Because of the proximity of different ethnic groups, however, Ivorians are, of necessity, becoming multilingual.

Religion

Over 60 percent of the population of Côte d'Ivoire continues to honor beliefs and religious practices similar to those that are found throughout much of sub-Saharan Africa. In addition, many Ivorians also accept the presence of a universal life force as part of the natural order. In rural areas —where people are not heavily influenced by other religions—this belief is still the major focus of people's religious lives.

ISLAM
Islam originated in seventh-century Arabia, where the inspired prophet Muhammad first spread the doctrine of the Koran, or holy writings. Today Islam is

the second largest religion in the world and in Africa alone claims 125 million believers, called Muslims.

Islam came to West Africa in three waves. Berbers brought the faith to the Ghana Empire in the ninth century A.D. From the thirteenth to the eighteenth centuries, some Malinke sovereigns spread Islam throughout the savanna region that formed a border of the Mali Empire. Islam continued to grow in Côte d'Ivoire under the influence of the armed forces of Samory Touré, whose brief passage across the country's northern savannas intimidated many local people into temporarily accepting Islam.

In the twentieth century various Islamic revival movements have contributed to the integration of this religion into the lives of Ivorians. In modern times, rural Ivorians have viewed Islam as an African religion. Muslims compose almost a quarter of the nation's population, binding a variety of ethnic groups into a single, strong religious community.

CHRISTIANITY

Fourteen percent of the population, mostly in the southern cities, belongs to various Christian religions. Christianity tends to be the religion of the educated middle class and of the elite. Unlike Islam, orthodox Christianity is seen as an alien religion and is viewed suspiciously by rural Ivorians.

In 1914 the Liberian prophet William Wade Harris spread Christianity in Côte d'Ivoire. He traveled along the lagoon-spotted coast preaching about the Christian God. Ivorians were attracted by his simple, holy life and religious zeal, and over 120,000 of them were personally baptized by Harris.

Harrism, though basically a form of fundamental Christianity, is viewed by many Ivorians as an African religion since it was taught by an African rather than by white European or U.S. missionaries. Though opposed by both Protestant and Catholic missionaries, the Harrist Church continues to gain followers in urban areas of Côte d'Ivoire.

Literature

Ivorian literature in the French language began with a short comedy, *Les villes*, written in 1933 by Bernard Dadié. A later play by Dadié, *Assemien Dehle*, was produced in Paris in 1937 at the Théâtre des Champs-Elysées. Dadié has also written novels and short stories. Another leading writer is François-Joseph Amon d'Aby, who is not only a playwright but also the author of serious studies of various as-

A Harrist church, whose founder was the Liberian prophet William Wade Harris, is located in the Blokosso section of Abidjan.

Independent Picture Service

Faithful Muslims are required to pray five times each day facing toward the city of Mecca in Saudi Arabia, where Muhammad—Islam's great prophet—was born.

pects of Ivorian life. One of his best-known plays is *Kwua Adjoba*.

Other writers are the novelists Aké Loba, Zègona Gbessi Nokan, and Amadou Koné and the short-story writer Raphaël Atta Koffi. Anthropologist B. Holas is the author of numerous works dealing with African, and particularly Ivorian, art and culture. Among these are *L'Homme noir d'Afrique* (The black man of Africa), *Arts traditionnels de la Côte d'Ivoire,* and *Les Senoufo.*

Music and Dance

All public functions include music. When the occasion is ceremonial, the music is usually performed strictly according to pre-established forms. Most of the music resounding throughout Côte d'Ivoire, how-

ever, is social and not ceremonial in nature. No distinction exists between audience and performers; music, therefore, is very spontaneous. Everyone participates—by humming, singing, clapping, or playing an instrument.

The drum is the universal instrument in Africa. Côte d'Ivoire has drums of all sizes and shapes. Drumming is considered a fine art among some groups, and masters of the art develop rhythms that are impressively complex. Another traditional Ivorian instrument is a wooden xylophone called a balaphon, which is common in the north, especially among the Senufo.

In the coastal cities of West Africa, creative musicians have successfully blended traditional rhythms and U.S. black music to form a new and distinctive style that is tremendously popular among Ivorian

41

These goldsmiths produce jewelry using the cire perdue (lost-wax) process. The craftsmen form wax models of the jewelry and coat them with clay to make a mold. After heating the wax until it melts and escapes from holes in the molds, the goldsmiths pour liquid metal into the space left vacant by the wax.

young people. Afrobeat—as the new music is called—brings together electric guitars, saxophones, horns, and a variety of percussion instruments.

While dancing, too, is often a spontaneous social activity, the most outstanding dances of Côte d'Ivoire occur as part of established ceremonies and events. Many ceremonial dances are quite theatrical, involving elaborate and vivid costumes and masks. The dances of the region of Man are characterized by acrobatic maneuvers and potentially dangerous stunts.

Traditional Crafts

Côte d'Ivoire has long been famous for the quality of its art, including some of the most intricate wood carvings in all of Africa. Originally, most Ivorian art objects were masks or statues created for ceremonial occasions. These same objects are produced today in greater numbers for sale to tourists and collectors. For each ethnic group, art objects are created within traditional, cultural patterns. An artwork, therefore, is more an expression of a culture than of an individual.

As a group, the Baule are especially artistic and produce artworks not only for ceremony but also for the satisfaction of creating things of beauty. Baule homes are often graced by carved doors and furniture, as well as by numerous decorative objects. The statues and masks of the Senufo emphasize human or animal

Photo by Tourisme Côte d'Ivoire

Carved masks are among the most unique artworks in Côte d'Ivoire. Some have a ritual significance *(above)*, and others demonstrate the skill of the artist *(right)*.

Courtesy of George Peery

Photo by Tourisme Côte d'Ivoire

Dances of the Man region are often dangerously acrobatic. Here, two men juggle a young girl on drawn knives.

features in startling, nightmarish fashions. The style developed by the Senufo is considered one of the most important contributions to African art. Besides wood carving and sculpture, the peoples of Côte d'Ivoire are very much involved in pottery making, painting, and fashioning objects of gold.

Education

About one-third of recent Ivorian budgets have been devoted to education. In the mid-1980s over 892,000 students attended primary schools, and more than 43,000 students went to secondary schools. Although attendance is not compulsory, 75 percent of Ivorian children go to classes.

A sandal maker produces his sturdy, leather wares on the streets of Treichville.

Courtesy of United Nations

44

Carrying her stool on her head, a young Ivorian reluctantly prepares to go to school.

Côte d'Ivoire has made great progress toward assuring primary education for most children. The secondary system also has been extended since the nation gained independence. As students advance, the government offers incentives—such as full scholarships and a living allowance—to continue their education at the university level.

The University of Abidjan is the major branch of the National University of Côte d'Ivoire. Founded in 1963, the university has a current enrollment of about 11,500 students, including some 8,500 Ivorians. Its five faculties teach courses in science, medicine, economics, law, and letters.

Besides the university, a number of specialized institutes with courses in teacher training, engineering, business, the arts, and public administration are found in the Cocody district of Abidjan.

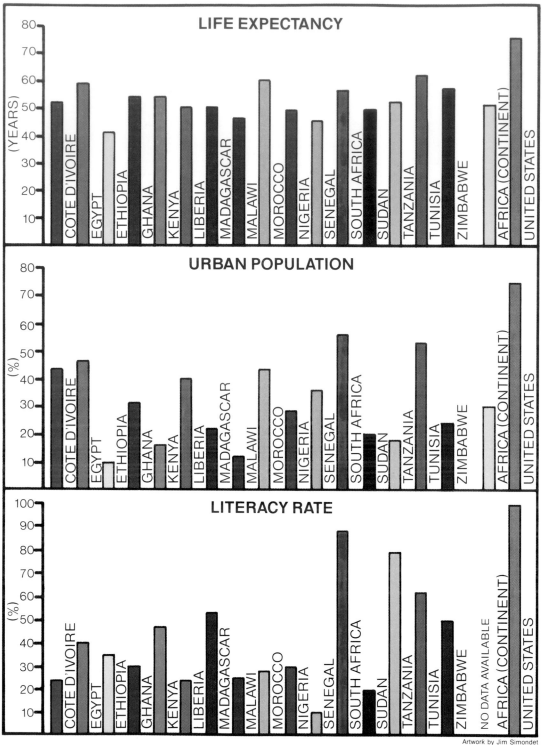

LIFE EXPECTANCY

(YEARS)

COTE D'IVOIRE
EGYPT
ETHIOPIA
GHANA
KENYA
LIBERIA
MADAGASCAR
MALAWI
MOROCCO
NIGERIA
SENEGAL
SOUTH AFRICA
SUDAN
TANZANIA
TUNISIA
ZIMBABWE
AFRICA (CONTINENT)
UNITED STATES

URBAN POPULATION

(%)

COTE D'IVOIRE
EGYPT
ETHIOPIA
GHANA
KENYA
LIBERIA
MADAGASCAR
MALAWI
MOROCCO
NIGERIA
SENEGAL
SOUTH AFRICA
SUDAN
TANZANIA
TUNISIA
ZIMBABWE
AFRICA (CONTINENT)
UNITED STATES

LITERACY RATE

(%)

COTE D'IVOIRE
EGYPT
ETHIOPIA
GHANA
KENYA
LIBERIA
MADAGASCAR
MALAWI
MOROCCO
NIGERIA
SENEGAL
SOUTH AFRICA
SUDAN
TANZANIA
TUNISIA
ZIMBABWE
NO DATA AVAILABLE
AFRICA (CONTINENT)
UNITED STATES

Artwork by Jim Simondet

The three factors depicted in this graph suggest differences in the quality of life among 16 African nations. Averages for the United States and the entire continent of Africa are included for comparison. Data taken from "1987 World Population Data Sheet" and *PC-Globe.*

A wide variety of research institutions—jointly financed by Côte d'Ivoire and France—study coffee, cacao, rubber, cotton, oils and oil-producing plants, forestry, and marine life. The institutes try to determine the varieties, growing conditions, pest control methods, and efficient production techniques that will increase agricultural output.

Health

While public health standards in Côte d'Ivoire compare well with those of nearby countries, they are still low in comparison to the standards of industrialized nations. Overcrowding, inadequate water and sewage facilities, and lack of health education all combine to create a widespread sanitation problem that is the major obstacle to high standards of public health in urban areas.

In extremely impoverished areas, especially in the northern savanna region, nutritional deficiencies contribute to poor health. The farm families of this region live mainly on millet and rice and, therefore, lack some essential proteins and vitamins in their diet.

Where inadequate sanitation exists and where nutritional deficiencies are common, poorer Ivorians easily contract diseases. Many die each year of malaria and other parasitic diseases and of pneumonia and tuberculosis. The average life expectancy in the nation is about 52 years—an average rate for Africa, but low when compared to countries of the West.

To supplement diets that are poor in nutritional content, the government, with the help of international agencies, encourages the production of smoked fish *(left)*, which will be edible for a longer time than freshly caught seafood. The growing of citrus fruits, such as pineapples *(below)*, is also encouraged to boost nutritional quality.

The Ministry of Public Health controls regional diseases—such as yellow fever—by providing mass vaccinations. Modern hospitals have been established in Abidjan and Bouaké, and mobile units bring health education and treatment to the outlying areas. The infant mortality rate—105 deaths in every 1,000 live births—is high but not for Africa, where the average figure is 113 deaths per 1,000 births.

The World Health Organization (WHO) is coordinating research, education, and treatment for AIDS—acquired immune deficiency syndrome. Insufficient health information and substandard medical facilities have contributed to the spread of this epidemic disease. By mid-1987 only 118 cases had been reported in Côte d'Ivoire, but WHO suspects that unreported incidences of the disease may affect two million people throughout the African continent.

Independent Picture Service

The leaders of a Wobe village in western Côte d'Ivoire share a meal of *fufu*. The dish can be made of yams, plantains (bananalike fruits), cassava (a fleshy root), millet, or corn flour and is enjoyed throughout West Africa. Fufu is usually eaten with spicy sauces made from available foods, such as peppers or peanuts.

Independent Picture Service

A variety of freshly grown produce is offered at a busy Ivorian street market.

Food

Staple foods in Côte d'Ivoire include yams, plantains (large bananalike fruits), rice, millet, and peanuts. The emphasis on these foods varies in different places. In the northern savanna region, for example, rice with a peppery peanut sauce is a common dish. Closer to the coast, fish served with fried plantains is popular.

Fufu, the national dish of Côte d'Ivoire, is made by pounding plantains, cassavas, or yams to form a sticky dough. The dough is then served with a highly seasoned meat sauce. Fufu is eaten by hand, and the process of securing a fingerful of dough, dipping it in the sauce, and popping it into the mouth can be a challenging maneuver for a beginner.

A cook at an elementary school at Abobo Baoule, near Abidjan, prepares the day's meal with produce from the school's garden.

4) The Economy

In the late 1970s and early 1980s Côte d'Ivoire was spurred toward progress by one of the fastest growing and most energetic economies in Africa. The gross national product (GNP) almost quadrupled between 1960 and 1975. The average income per person in 1984 was $1,100 per year, one of the highest in Africa.

This remarkable economic growth resulted from agricultural expansion and from improvements in farming methods and equipment. The development of the forestry industry and a dramatic boom in Ivorian export industries also contributed to the upturn in revenue.

The present economy of Côte d'Ivoire is the result of long-range planning by Houphouët-Boigny and his advisers. When Houphouët-Boigny became chief executive in 1960, Côte d'Ivoire was blessed with many potentially valuable natural resources but enjoyed very little income. Most major financial transactions occurred with France.

Houphouët-Boigny believed that, in order to attract the money necessary to stimulate the Ivorian economy, he had to create a good investment climate. As a result of that belief, the president enacted tax exemptions and encouraged a governmental attitude that sought to ensure profits for investors. Houphouët-Boigny channeled into agriculture—the most basic sector of the economy—the foreign money that first trickled and then poured into Côte d'Ivoire.

Agriculture

Agriculture—the livelihood of most Ivorians—accounts for more than 80 percent of the exports of Côte d'Ivoire. The economic success in agriculture is due in part to the deepwater port at Abidjan and to the well-developed road network, both of which make it easy to transport products quickly to African markets and to other parts of the world.

Two major crops—coffee and cacao—account for nearly 75 percent of the nation's total exports. In 1986 Côte d'Ivoire was the world's largest producer of cacao, the world's third largest producer of coffee, and the fourth largest producer of pineapples.

A palm oil plantation is seen from a roadside near Bingerville. Côte d'Ivoire was once the world's third largest exporter of palm oil. Aging plantations have weakened the country's lead in the market, inspiring the government to launch a major palm oil rehabilitation and expansion program.

The latter have been cultivated seriously only since 1950. Côte d'Ivoire is also the leading cultivator of bananas in Africa and ranks among the top 10 producers of this fruit in the world.

Houphouët-Boigny realized early that if an economy depends too heavily on two or three export crops, it will suffer severe setbacks when international market prices fall. Consequently, he enacted a scheme of agricultural expansion in 1962. Experimental crops were planted, and some of them have flourished in recent years.

Palm oil, which has long been an essential ingredient in the preparation of African food, was originally produced from wild palm trees for local use. In the early 1960s the trees began to be cultivated for export. By the mid-1980s Côte d'Ivoire was the world's leading exporter of this product.

The cultivation of rubber trees, which began on a limited scale in 1956, is beginning to pay dividends in the 1980s. Two large, new plantations have been established in the southwest. International banks financed the development, and the Michelin (France) and Goodyear (United States) tire companies provided technical assistance.

Cotton was cultivated on a small scale from 1930 to 1960, but production has skyrocketed since 1960, when new growing methods were introduced. Much of the nation's raw cotton is used to supply Côte d'Ivoire's own textile mills. Other export

A group of agricultural laborers harvests a field of rice—a staple crop in West Africa.

A plantation worker picks cotton—an important farm product in Côte d'Ivoire—while the child slung from her back helps with the task.

Only recently have Côte d'Ivoire's deposits of petroleum been explored. This offshore platform is located 15 miles from the Ivorian coast in the Gulf of Guinea.

crops currently being developed are coconuts, rice, sugarcane, and tobacco.

Natural Resources

Fertile soil and an abundant water supply have traditionally been the chief natural resources of Côte d'Ivoire. In the 1970s, however, foreign petroleum producers began offshore explorations and found sufficient deposits to warrant the construction of drilling complexes. The ESSO firm and its partners brought the Belier field into production in 1980, and a larger field —called Espoir (Hope)—began production in 1982.

The collapse of world oil prices, however, has endangered the petroleum-producing sector of the Ivorian economy. Moreover, output from the two fields—only about 21,000 barrels annually—is declining because of lack of further investment. On the other hand, the low oil prices have stimulated the Abidjan oil refinery's production. Thus Côte d'Ivoire is about 85 percent self-sufficient in crude oil. The refinery has a four-million-ton capacity, which meets domestic requirements and allows for exports to neighboring nations, such as Burkina Faso and Mali.

The only other mineral resources extracted commercially are diamonds and manganese, both in relatively small quantities. Surveys have established the possibility of mining iron ore, gold, bauxite (unprocessed aluminum), and lithium (a soft metal). Definite plans to exploit these resources await improvements in world prices.

Forestry

The southern half of Côte d'Ivoire once was covered with more than 12 million acres of thick forest. Although the timber

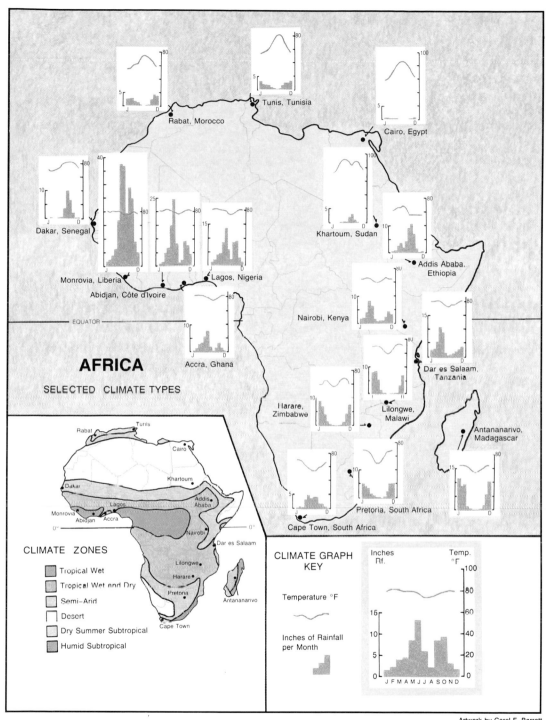

AFRICA

SELECTED CLIMATE TYPES

Rabat, Morocco

Tunis, Tunisia

Cairo, Egypt

Dakar, Senegal

Khartoum, Sudan

Addis Ababa, Ethiopia

Monrovia, Liberia

Abidjan, Côte d'Ivoire

Lagos, Nigeria

Accra, Ghana

EQUATOR

Nairobi, Kenya

Dar es Salaam, Tanzania

Harare, Zimbabwe

Lilongwe, Malawi

Antananarivo, Madagascar

Pretoria, South Africa

Cape Town, South Africa

CLIMATE ZONES

Tunis
Rabat
Cairo
Khartoum
Dakar
Addis Ababa
Lagos
Monrovia
Abidjan Accra
Nairobi
Dar es Salaam
Lilongwe
Harare
Pretoria
Antananarivo
Cape Town

0°

CLIMATE ZONES

Tropical Wet
Tropical Wet and Dry
Semi-Arid
Desert
Dry Summer Subtropical
Humid Subtropical

CLIMATE GRAPH KEY

Inches Rf.
Temp. °F

Temperature °F

Inches of Rainfall per Month

J F M A M J J A S O N D

Artwork by Carol F. Barrett

These climate graphs show the monthly change in the average rainfall received and in the average temperature from January to December for the capital cities of 16 African nations. On the graph for Abidjan, Côte d'Ivoire, little variation in temperature exists between summer and winter. Although Abidjan is classified as having a tropical wet climate, substantial differences occur in monthly rainfall totals, and at least four months are relatively dry. Data taken from *World-Climates* by Willy Rudloff, Stuttgart, 1981.

55

industry began slowly with the exportation of mahogany, it has grown as new, usable species have been discovered and exploited. In the mid-1970s timber surpassed coffee as the principal export. To process the timber, more sawmills and other wood-processing operations have been established. These facilities produce plywood, veneers, crates, boxes, cabinets, and furniture.

The entire forestry industry is regulated by the Ministry of Water and Forest Resources, whose original objective was to conserve and increase forest reserves. Unfortunately, poor management and over-cutting have resulted in a decline in forestry and forest products in the 1980s. Today Côte d'Ivoire faces severe problems of deforestation and soil erosion.

Industry

In order to expand its economic base and to become more self-sufficient, Côte d'Ivoire—helped by foreign investors—poured considerable energy and money into various domestic and export industries. For domestic use, factories sprang up in Abidjan and Bouaké that processed and packaged milk products, soda, cigarettes,

Mahogany logs, cut from dwindling forest reserves in Côte d'Ivoire, are loaded at the port of Abidjan for export to Europe and North America.

Improvements in cotton-growing techniques have expanded the Ivorian textile industry.

At a factory in Bouaké, a worker runs a machine that processes cigarettes.

The deepwater port at San Pedro in southwestern Côte d'Ivoire was the first step in an ambitious development plan for the area.

matches, soap, and many other everyday items. Even automobile and radio assembly plants have begun to operate in Bouaké.

In order to reduce regional economic differences, a sugar refinery was established in the relatively poor savanna region in the north. The refinery, situated in Ferkessédougou, was built with U.S. money and technical support and was supposed to have an output capacity of 60,000 tons per year. Unfortunately, poor management, insufficient sugarcane production, and high costs have virtually closed this plant.

For the first 20 years of its independence, Côte d'Ivoire's progress appeared astounding—the nation's economy grew by an average of about 6 percent each year. In the early 1980s, however, government expenses began to exceed income. The country's borrowing to finance poorly planned ventures, as well as the decline in timber production, forced the government to take out huge foreign loans. The rising international debt and falling export receipts led to a recession through the mid-1980s. Consequently, government investments in major industries have had to be cut back severely.

Ambitious Projects

In the 1970s, as part of its long-range economic plan, Côte d'Ivoire engaged in two ambitious projects of great social and economic importance. The first project was the construction of the Kossou hydroelectric dam on the Bandama River near Yamoussoukro. The cost of the project was $170 million; three-fourths of this amount was spent on the actual construction of the dam. The remainder was used to transfer 75,000 people, whose homes were flooded when the water level rose.

At peak efficiency, the dam was to produce 500 million kilowatts, which would have equaled the power production of the entire country. Unfortunately, insufficient water reserves have never allowed the dam to function at full capacity. Other benefits of the project also have never been realized. For example, a greater volume of water would have allowed large expanses of land to be irrigated, thus increasing crop yields of coffee, cacao, and rice. In addition, a tourist center on artificial Lake Kossou never has materialized.

The second project, Operation San Pedro, was a three-part development plan that was dramatically to change southwestern Côte d'Ivoire. The project included the construction of a deepwater port capable of handling freighters and liners, as well as the building of a town providing housing and facilities for 25,000 inhabitants. In addition, a 300-mile road network was planned that would connect Daloa to the new coastal town at San Pedro. Operation San Pedro, which is still unfinished, has already cost more than $58 million and has resulted in massive Ivorian debts to Italy, France, and West Germany. Developers hoped the planned site would improve communication and transportation, as well

Courtesy of Tom O'Toole

One of Côte d'Ivoire's most promising construction projects was the building of the Kossou hydroelectric complex. Located near Yamoussoukro on the Bandama River, the plant has yet to reach peak capacity.

as help to exploit agricultural and forestry resources that had not been fully tapped. But the hopes for the project have yet to be fulfilled.

Tourism

The tourist industry, though nonagricultural, has proved sensitive to changes in the world economy. European investors have profited more than Ivorians have from the development of the tourist trade.

The once-elegant, 750-room Hôtel Ivoire in Abidjan exemplifies the Ivorian government's enthusiasm for promoting tourism. The hotel contains seven restaurants, several swimming pools, a casino, a golf course, and the only ice-skating rink in tropical Africa.

Highlights of the tourist industry in Côte d'Ivoire are the elaborate seaside resorts that have been established in the last few years at coastal locations such as Assinie. The grandest and most ambitious experiment in tourism in West Africa, however, is the "African Riviera," which occupies 10,000 acres of coastal lagoons to the east of Abidjan. Plans for the project involve the construction of a city for 120,000 inhabitants, an international exhibition complex, plush and varied accommodations, and entertainment facilities. All of these amenities—plus a Disneyland-type amusement park and an animal reserve—remain in the planning stages.

Transportation

Côte d'Ivoire has one of the best developed road networks in West Africa. There are 28,336 miles of paved roads, more than one-half of which are usable throughout the year. Privately owned buses transport Ivorians between cities.

The Abidjan-Niger Railway runs down the middle of Côte d'Ivoire, covering the 700-mile stretch between Abidjan and

Abidjan's Hôtel Ivoire—the centerpiece of the Côte d'Ivoire's tourism facilities—has over 700 rooms and recreational facilities that include several swimming pools and West Africa's only ice-skating rink.

Travelers board a train—part of the
Abidjan-Niger Railway—that will take
them to Bouaké.

Courtesy of United Nations

Independent Picture Service

Côte d'Ivoire has an excellent overland transportation network. A modern bridge and connecting highway link the Plateau
in Abidjan to the suburb of Treichville.

Abidjan's port facilities are among the most complete in French-speaking West Africa.

Ouagadougou, the capital of Burkina Faso. A host of international airlines service Côte d'Ivoire through Abidjan's Port-Bouët Airport, which is fully equipped to handle jet traffic. Nine other airports are situated across Côte d'Ivoire and are maintained by Air Ivoire, the national airline.

The port of Abidjan is the largest in French-speaking Africa. There are 14 wharves for docking, loading, and storage, as well as extensive warehouse facilities. The port accommodates international passenger liners and freighters.

Outlook for the Future

While the growing economy of Côte d'Ivoire has greatly improved the quality of life of some citizens, it also, inevitably, has created problems. Gross financial in-

The rapid urbanization of Ivorian society—reflected in the modern skyline of Abidjan—has created social and cultural tensions within Côte d'Ivoire.

equality exists in Côte d'Ivoire, and a very small percentage of the population—mostly those of European origin—controls much of the spendable income. Top management positions in business and industry are usually filled by Europeans, and many Ivorians feel that this arrangement is unjust.

In 1962 Houphouët-Boigny began a policy of ivorization—that is, of bringing the financial and industrial management of Côte d'Ivoire into the hands of Ivorians. The president felt that ivorization was essential but believed that it had to be accomplished gradually, never at the risk of industrial competence or economic growth. To this end, the government paid for the training of Ivorians for high-level positions and lent financial aid to Ivorian entrepreneurs. Since 1972 non-Ivorian professionals—such as doctors and lawyers—have been forbidden to open new practices.

Another problem results from the rapid urbanization process that the society is experiencing. Abidjan grew from a population of 180,000 in 1960 to over 2 million in 1987. Rapid urbanization has led to unemployment and to problems of housing and crime. The family—the social institution around which traditional life has revolved—is undergoing severe stress as increasing numbers of young people leave their villages for the city.

Ivorians must combine the values of urban and rural lifestyles if they are to lead productive lives. Moreover, they need to be prepared to face the political and economic challenges that will result after the inevitable departure of Côte d'Ivoire's aging president.

President Houphouët-Boigny (left foreground), who is in his eighties, has created a governmental structure that requires his presence. How Côte d'Ivoire will cope with its future after the president's departure from the political scene is the cause of some concern within the nation.

Index